preface

In late January 2006, my friend Mark Cunningham called to tell me that one of the bands his company managed was looking for a "t-shirt guy." I'd been spinning my wheels in upstate New York, having seemingly run out of options other than going back to school. The timing was perfect. The tour would start in mid-March and run through the second week of April, right around the time I would be sweating bullets over graduate school applications. I asked Mark if I could bring my camera on the road. Sure, he said, why not? The band's first single, "Over My Head (Cable Car)," was catching on, and the band's monitor engineer, Brian, had been shooting video of the crowds singing along every night. Mark suggested I could probably take over for him.

A few weeks later, I found myself flying into a cold and rainy St. Louis, entirely unsure as to what the next three weeks on the road had in store. Other than several hectic coast-to-coast moves, I'd never had the time to actually get out on the road and explore. Would I get my own bunk? Did the beds have sheets? What about power outlets? And where would I go to the bathroom? From the minute I landed in Missouri I started filming: my taxi ride from the airport, my arrival at the Pageant Theatre, the bus parked in the empty sleet-drenched parking lot behind the venue.

As I wandered in the backstage door, I came face-to-face with the guys. Introductions were made and I tried to imagine who played which instrument. It was Thursday, March 23rd, the start of the band's second head-lining tour, a three-week stint around the Midwest. Every show on our run would sell out. To say the rise was meteoric would be an understatement.

That first night at the Pageant, I snuck away from the merchandise table. Though I probably wasn't supposed to, though I could have lost my job for leaving the merchandise unattended, I got my camera out and started shooting. When it came time to settle with the venue that night, the cash box was around a hundred dollars under, the only time it would be short during my days as the cotton tech.

We woke up the next day in dreary Kansas City, and I went about setting up my merchandise stand. I managed to find time to shoot more footage of the band as they took care of the few hours of boredom that come mid-afternoon in an empty rock club, the sound check, a trip up the street to a mediocre burrito stand, and then some more of the show. I was taking liberties, certainly, but nobody took much notice. A few days later, Ben and Joe asked to see some of the footage I'd been shooting. It was that moment that solidified my creative relationship with the band and became the catalyst that would eventually send me off on the journey of documenting nearly ever step of The Fray's existence over the next three years.

Several weeks ago I asked Isaac if I could get a ride home from the studio. Production for the band's second album was coming to an end, and I was hoping to squeeze off a few more shots of the dusky Denver sky-line for the studio documentary I'd been shooting for the past five months. Halfway home, Isaac turned to me and asked if I liked any of the songs. For a few short breaths I considered his question. "I love them all," I said. "How could I not?" After spending so much time with the band, I felt an indescribable connection to the unique existence of four musicians whose moments felt more and more like my own. Having been there every step of the way, over three hundred shows, thousands of frequent-flyer miles, countless stamps in my passport, and just as many photographs, it was hard not to feel the emotional attachment to each and every moment. This had become my life and these new songs a testament and soundtrack to every single one of my images.

The photographs printed on these pages are a simple documenta-tion of existence: from naps caught in a dressing room in Switzerland to the thousand eager faces at a show in Minneapolis. To me these images represent more than just a year of travel, tour, and life. They are a living record, proof that all of this has actually happened. These moments are not just memories. Life in a band and being on the road is like everything and nothing you would imagine. It is both beautiful and brutal. But if you ever went looking for proof as to the size of Ben, Joe, David, and Isaac's hearts and the passion for what they do, perhaps it would be found within these pages.

Rod Blackhurst
September 5, 2008

DTE ENERGY MUSIC CENTER
CLARKSTON, MI

Lunch	12:30 PM
The Fray Soundcheck	3:00 PM
Support Line Check	4:30 PM
Dinner	5:30 PM
Doors Open	7:00 PM
Mae	7:30 PM
Set Change	7:45 PM
OK Go	8:30 PM
Set Change	9:00 PM
The Fray	11:00 PM
Curfew	AFTER LOAD OUT
Legend	

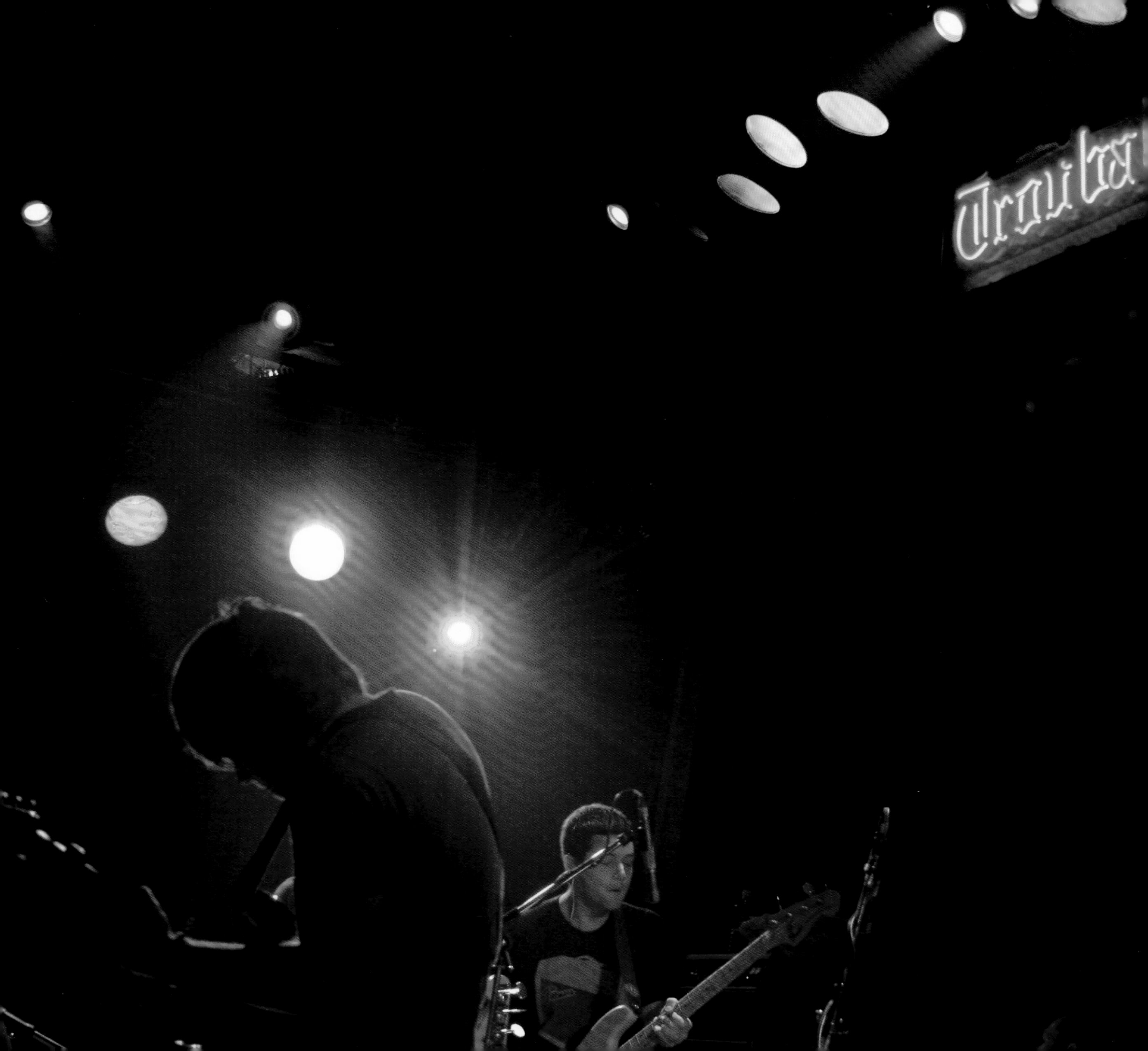

I often succumb to reflection, lapsing into introspection not entirely will-ingly but because of a real awareness of the life we have led ourselves into. And this awareness does not necessarily uncover a willful trepidation on our parts—a "brave new world" mentality that we were unquestionably made for. No, the awareness is made present through the evidence of road rash, our weathering over these past years. This is not meant to sound glamorous, or even masculine in a sense, like the look of a tarnished pair of boots or the personality of an old pair of jeans. The honest nature is in the long, strained nights in deep conversation; the attempt at communica-tion across at least one ocean through an abyss of wireless "convenience"; the realization, upstairs in a tepid green room in a midwestern college town club, that your "art" feels more like speed drills on a hot August afternoon. Confronting the notion that, perhaps in the eyes of some, you have become simply a product, a piece of merchandise on the shelves of mega-mall electronics stores.

However, as introspection so often allows conflicting emotions to frustratingly coexist, I must examine the reflection: the nostalgia in recall-ing hurried travel through airports, train stations, subways, and suffocat-ingly crowded sidewalks; the blessing that is a croissant and strong cup of *café* from a patisserie amid an awakening Paris; the exhilaration cours-ing through the body as twenty thousand people sing along to a song conceived in a living room; and, though simple in concept, the humanistic connection between two people tied loosely through a shared artful experience.

We began accumulating Polaroid pictures before we entered the studio over three years ago. A wall of these square, framed images took form in a sleepy town in Indiana when we stayed there through the dreary months of February and March. Shoeboxes were filled; Isaac, a packrat by nature, was running low on available storage space. It wasn't long before we found ourselves on a bus for the first time—the duality, the disharmony, the cold bunks!—and not long after that, a young man with ambition bubbling through his pores assumed the humble position of merchandise salesman. Strangely, he always traveled with three cameras.

Rod, in the most complimentary sense of the word, became invisible. He became increasingly adept at being neither seen nor heard, yet cap-turing more memorable images than our memory served us and often serving us a bellyful of laughter with unassuming faces and nonchalant idiocy.

The past must be revered, and yet in reverence idolatry thrives. In this place, this paradoxical approach to reminiscence, we keep our prag-matism. We remember the difficult evenings, lackluster performances, and embittered disagreements. And so this book exists not simply as another product to file alphabetically, or a haughty demonstration of an established fiction; it is an extension of the art itself, encompassing boldly the connotations and implications, both fulfilling and deprecating. It is the visualization of the passage of time for people so uniquely con-nected. It will, hopefully, aid in a reflection that begins with association.

David Welsh
February 16, 2008

DEAR SARAH:

THANKS FOR THE LETTER.
THIS IS THE FIRST TIME WE
HAVE WRITTEN BACK TO
A FAN LETTER.

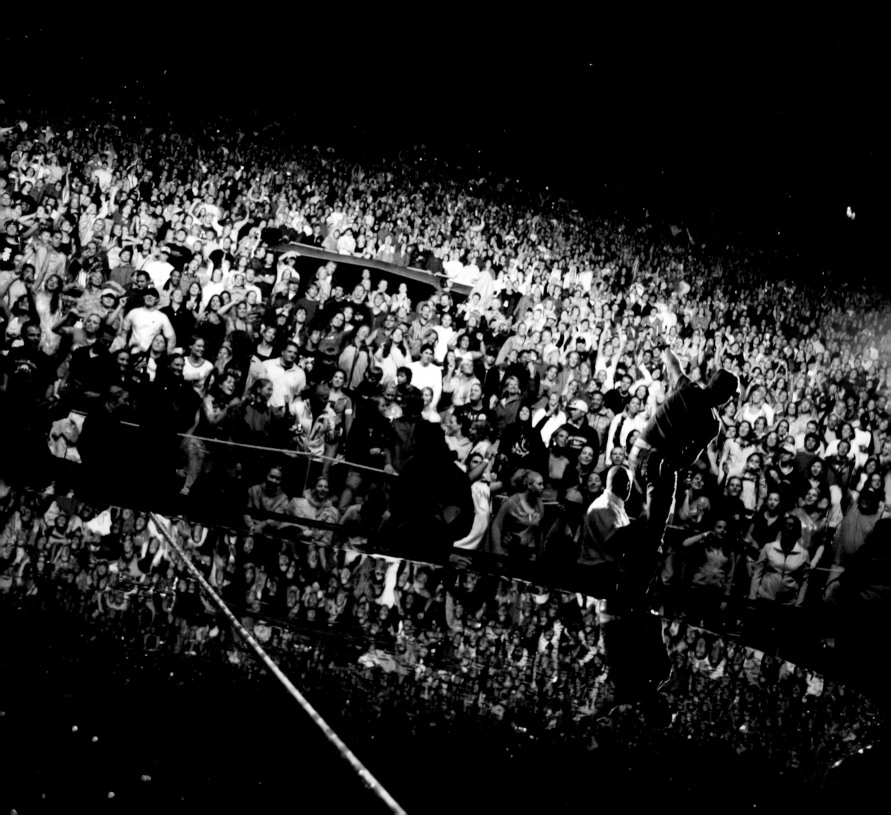

To all the touring and studio crew:
Mark Maher
Stephen Clark
Brian Joseph
Dan Lavery
Jonathan Parker
Jeff Linsenmaier
Joel Wojcik
Joel Forman
Allyson Fief
Jimmy Stofer
Chris Messina
Andrew Miller
Mike Flynn
Aaron Johnson
Warren Huart
Seth Kent
Beamon Lawrence
Jerry Henderson

Management and label:
Gregg Latterman
Jason Rio
Josh Terry
Reid Hunter
Jonathan Adelman
Lillian Williams
Tiffany Wiggers
Scott Carter
Calvin Aurand
Sarah Joyce
Lina Finelli
Doug McVehil
Jason Ienner

Larry, Mary, Wilson + Kelly Blackhurst
Matthew Jordan
Alex Dezen
Matt Hales
Kelly Magelky
Alan Schaefer
Clint Baker

In Loving Memory of Miles Parker
For Jonathan + Tanya Parker

The Fray is Joe King, Isaac Slade,
David Welsh, and Ben Wysocki

The Fray: There & Back
First Edition 2009

Published by Fancy's Show Books LLC, Denver, CO

Library of Congress Control Number: 2008940700
ISBN: 978-0-615-22944-7

Designed by John Hubbard
Copyedited by Marissa Meyer
Color management by iocolor, Seattle
Produced by Marquand Books, Inc., Seattle
    www.marquand.com
Printed and bound in China by Asia Pacific Offset